There Is No Place Without You

poems

Maya Bernstein

Ben Yehuda Press
Teaneck, New Jersey

Published by Ben Yehuda Press
122 Ayers Court #1B
Teaneck, NJ 07666

http://www.BenYehudaPress.com

To subscribe to our monthly book club and support independent Jewish publishing, visit https://www.patreon.com/BenYehudaPress

Jewish Poetry Project #27   http://jpoetry.us

Ben Yehuda Press books may be purchased at a discount by synagogues, book clubs, and other institutions buying in bulk. For information, please email markets@BenYehudaPress.com

Cover image by tropicalpixsingapore/iStockPhoto

ISBN13 978-1-953829-32-0

Library of Congress Cataloging-in-Publication Data

Names: Bernstein, Maya, author.
Title: There is no place without you : poems / Maya Bernstein.
Description: Teaneck, New Jersey : Ben Yehuda Press, [2022] | Series:
  Jewish poetry project ; 27 | Summary: "Poems exploring the gaping space
  between the infinitude of the divine and the finite nature of human
  existence"-- Provided by publisher.
Identifiers: LCCN 2022024898 | ISBN 9781953829320 (paperback)
Subjects: LCGFT: Poetry.
Classification: LCC PS3602.E762854 T47 2022 | DDC 811/.6--dc23/eng/20220527
LC record available at https://lccn.loc.gov/2022024898

22 23 24 / 10 9 8 7 6 5 4 3 2 1   202220814

for Noam

In a back courtyard of the world
we played, he and I.

I covered my eyes, he
hid: one, two, three —

not in front, not behind,
not inside.

Ever since then I've been searching
        for so many years.

So what if I can't find you?
        Come out already, come out!
Can't you see that I give up?

Dan Pagis, "Hide and Seek"

Contents

years

An Hour

I walked with my son in the forest.

Nearly all the trees were bare

      except for one, golden-leaved,
      like a garlanded elder
      with a full head of hair.

Look, I said, *That tree*
is holding on
     for dear life
to all her leaves.

     No,
he said, *all those leaves*
     are clinging
           to that tree.

days

I'm Preparing My Body for Your Birth

the way the *Hevra Kadisha* prepares
the dead for burial.   I cut
my nails: thumb   pinky   middle-
finger   pointer   ring-
                    finger. I squeeze

my wedding band off that swollen
          stump. I anoint my massive
belly with lilac oil and watch the ghost
of your fist   move   across   me,
          a purple current

in that vast ocean I contain. Do the dead flutter
          so, too?   I squat
to stretch my pelvis, as narrow
as the ancient   gates
          of the Old   City

of Jerusalem, cool and wet, pilgrims
and peddlers coming   going
          squeezing   past
each other and the unseen
          spirits,

whose bodies, scrubbed and wrapped
in white   as mine is now, the towel barely
          stretching round,
                    are lowered down
as they rise   up—up—

I'm preparing my body to bear
          down   so you may rise, your
cry   as wild   and haunting
          as a Shofar's,
          so that the walls

Maya Bernstein

that separate you   from me
the living   from the dead
the holy   from the profane
    come crashing,
    crashing down.

What I Am Like When I Swim

I drop into the water,
      a diver
      off a hull in the night.

One moment a right angle with the wind
      the next, emptiness. Barely a ripple.

      Like falling into a dream. Last night I dreamt I was swimming,
      deep at the bottom of a pool. I needed to breathe
            so I took small breaths. Somehow, I was able to breathe
            in the water.

Today I backstroke back-and-forth, back-and-forth,
staring at the pale blue ceiling. My eyes are drawn
      to the round bronze clock
      on the starboard stone wall.

      Has that clock ever worked? Its second-
            hand tremors, a kind of phantom
                  limb, remembering the time when it could keep time.
      That is what I am like when I swim.
I lose the boundaries of my bones

      my toes trail fins,
            like long ribbons
                  on a mayflower pole. My neck grows
            gills, my tailbone a flipper, I become
                something shimmering
                    green, purple, blue, silver
            a flashing dorsal thing
                you cannot see
    that passes like a shadow,
            some tremor-thing, keeping time
              out of time,
                  my whole human body
              like a phantom limb of an elusive water beast.

Later, dripping, I struggle
to pull my woolen socks over my damp feet,
      remembering all those years when I couldn't reach
         past my protruding belly

full of water, blood, a swimming water
creature that would become
     an alive-thing. How I struggled
to pull the compression stockings
over my swollen calves!

      That creature is now my phantom
         limb, swimming in umbilical air
            as I keep returning and returning
        to the water.

I Begin Menopause When My Daughters Start Their Periods

Now my daughters bleed, bewildered,

shining. How childish of me to think in moon-time,

when it's the sun at the wheel, driving in years,

as my girls writhe in monthly moon-

pain in the back seat. And me up front, dry

windshield cracked, my foot on the gas —

Maya Bernstein

Welcome

Welcome to the midst of the mother that I am.
I can't deal with your Thunder Fear at 3 am.
It happens that I'm hoping, darling, daring, still.
      You will dream of lying in bed alone
as I once did. Hold on tight, for soon enough
this howling storm will rage in you.
It will blow right through you! And then
      you'll be just like me.
      You'll be just like me,
it will blow right through you and then
this howling storm will rage in you,
as I once did. Hold on. Tight. For soon enough
      you will dream of lying in bed alone.
It happens that I'm hoping, darling, daring. Still,
I can't deal with your Thunder Fear at 3am.
Welcome to the midst of the mother you'll become.

There Is No Place Without You

I wait patiently on the long line
to be admitted into the children's
zoo. Ticket limp in my sticky fingers.
I move slowly, behind a baby sleeping
in a blue stroller, ahead of a small girl
crying for a balloon animal, her quiet
older brother studying a ladybug with
his magnifying glass. The baby wakes.
I smile and play peek-a-boo. Now
it's my turn to enter. Past the duck
pond, stone turtles, rabbit-ear-rocks,
into the petting zoo. My mouth *Oh!*s,
my eyes tear, my legs buckle, my heart
drums to find you there, amidst the sheep,
the goats, the pecking chickens. To find you
waiting, approaching my outstretched hand,
your golden matted fur ragged as you avoid
the fifty-cent pellets, reach for my sleeve, grab
it with your teeth. A lion in a petting zoo
and no one seems to see you. You tug
at me. I pull back. You pull harder,
I relent, bury my face in your mangy mane.
No tickets required to leave, I whisper. You
fly, I cling to you. Windy sky. We arrive
at the pond at sunset. *I found you, I dared.
It's your turn now. Watch me
          swim. Tell me who I am.*
You sit in lion stillness. When I emerge,
dripping, you are gone. Sandy silence.
I wait for the moon to rise before returning
to the open waters. To search for you. Again.

Imprisoned in Repetition and Immanence
    – Simon de Beauvoir, *The Second Sex*

We're in the stream again today, my kids
      and I. They've stripped down to their underwear

to splash. Maternity can't rid
      me of ambition, but I'm imprisoned here,

in the park. Two perky local moms in yoga pants
      show up and warn us about the snapping

turtle. I snap at my kids to behave. I rant:
      Get out while you can! Your strapping

youth, strong glutes, and convictions will be devoured!
      They must be judging me. I smile and feel dumpy.

My kids fling rocks. I fling rocks. The hours
      are perpetuated without change. A century

passes. Why did I think I could produce something new?
I stare at my reflection in the stream, not knowing what I am, or who.

Watch Me Grow

My kindergartner comes home with a succulent.
       A minuscule popsicle flag bearing her beaming face
            is planted in its soil. "Watch me grow!" it states
in black sharpie in the cheery teacher's truculent

          nanoscopic handwriting vertically
     along the line of the stick; green chubby
thumb-print leaves jut from the messily
       painted pot. We place it on the sunny

       kitchen windowsill. Preoccupied, I skimp
on watering it. So why am I surprised when one
          by one the leaves lose their fluids, drop limp
off the stalk? I hope she doesn't notice.

    (She does). I wish she hadn't brought it home.
        But she had. We'll face what comes.

A Brief History of Puppy Sitting With Five Children

We puppy-sat Theo, our friends' floppy
Cavapoo. They said that he was trained. To
some extent he was: he didn't bark at night or pee

on the carpet. The kids knew
to wipe his paws and not to feed him dark chocolate.
They even filled his water bowl, but left the house

riddled with Lego rocketeers who ought
not be exposed to the roving black hole of his mouth.
The youngest noticed: *Theo took an astronaut!*

It was of course my job to enter the fraught
atmosphere of his expansive jaw, to reach
into the dark galaxy of tongue and teeth.

Slimy, stiff, intact: I somehow birthed it.
The kids orbited me and quipped: *Where's the helmet?*

Label Everything

You must label everything you send to camp –
  water bottles, goggles, each pair of underpants –

with your children's first and last names. In permanent marker,
  so it's clear who belongs to who. Character

traits are helpful too,
  so they can be traced back to you:

shy, loud, funny, proud
  jealous of an older brother, very, very mad

at mother, apt to throw a tantrum.
  History is also relevant: when

they were conceived, and where, and wanted, or unwanted,
  and if you have the space, predictions too are warranted:

likely to storm out of an older sister's wedding,
  unlikely to know where they are heading.

Sew it, iron it, use a sharpie, or tattoo
  it on their arms. Thread some red string through

from your heart to the hems of their shirts,
  and tie a knot or cut it clean. Either way, it will hurt.

Maya Bernstein

Into That Seat Still Warm With Her Older Sister's Presence

Every day: yesterday, today,
last Thursday, two Mondays ago,
when the older sister gets out
from the front passenger seat
of the van to go to high school,
even before the curt *bye*
from her lipsticked mouth
is murmured, she, the younger
sister, flings, from the back,
where she sits, to the floor
of the front, her back-pack,
jacket, drawstring bag with sports-bra
and basketball shoes, climbs over –
I'm moving to the front! –
and settles, for the four
minutes it takes
to drive to her school,
into that seat still warm
with her older sister's
presence. I sit at the red light,
my right blinker blinking
as I wait, watching,
as the older one gallops
across the street,
and the younger one
stares hard at the road ahead,
climbing into what she wants,
taking it, filling it
with who she is
in the time she has.
When she gets out,
she slams the door.
The wind swallows her
goodbye.

Walking to Synagogue on Yom Kippur,

in the unaltered neighborhood of my childhood
and I thought, *how I long to see*
an angel. I thought, *how I long to cross over*
into purity. Across the street,

a woman with her daughter
waved at me, and called out, *Maya, how are you*
and before I could recall her name, the daughter
said: *Who is Maya* and I thought, *She's not an angel.*

Again the girl said, *Who is Maya*
and I said, *that is the question*
I should be asking myself today,

and she kept asking, *Who is Maya,*
and I thought, *Maya*
means magic, or illusion in Sanskrit. Why
did my mother name me illusion
in Sanskrit? In synagogue

I recited the ancient words of the sacred prayer:
"Let us now relate the power of this day's holiness"

and thought
Was my mother an angel before I was born?
and said
"Angels will be frenzied"
and thought
that girl doesn't care who Maya is
and said
"A trembling and terror will seize them"
and thought,

that girl just wants to know how it is possible
her mother has a life that doesn't include her.

Mothering Means: Cease to Be {...} Become {...}

motherhood is a barrow

heaped with mounds
of dank earth

those piles of potential
that preoccupied me

before you came down like the rainwater

mothering means: cease to be {loam}
become {littered with your own debris}

weeks

Meditations on Incompatibility

Saturday, 8:14pm

There must be a better word than irony
(perhaps the Hungarian *gúny* - sarcasm, ridicule, mocking, taunting, jest)
to describe the experience of being immersed
in the last twenty pages of Imre Kertész's *Kaddish for an Unborn Child*
after having just spent the requisite nightly two hours
putting the younger ones to bed: dinner, baths, books, teeth,
toilet, the dark-eyed girl and headstrong boy,
            then the sneaking off
with one's tea to sit, to read, to escape
                an escape...an escape, indeed a salvation, a salvation
                and absolutely indispensable demonstration of myself...
but they smoke me out, the one putting her fingers in my hair,
the other bouncing a light-up ball, yet another relentlessly humming –
the noise of them deafening and Kertész's "No!" screeching
in my head like the young red-tailed hawk screeching
            all morning in the forest
swooping toward its prey and missing, screeching
in frustration, the goal just out of hand, just beyond grasp,
like me in my tree on my perch heavy with children
            (and Jewishness)
gazing hungrily at the flock of my might-have-beens,
narrowly escaped, flying free, now invisible in the bright sky

Maya Bernstein

Monday, 7:23am, in the Forest

something about the sound
of the wind slipping past my ears

    I could have been by Your sea

        foam and fresh and crest and salt and all

Tuesday, 4:30pm

An older daughter is in my attic space so I'm displaced.
I huddle at the corner of the dining room table and risk
being noticed (attacked). They're in the other room
testing my powers of concentration. The littlest one
screams at Babysitter from the bathroom: *I didn't poop!*
She calls back, *OK! So you don't need to!* I try
to wonder about a comma. Perhaps a parenthesis?
His slightly older sister says: *he just goes to the bathroom to play
with his penis, he loves his penis.* No rise from Babysitter
so sister continues, *I have a tiny penis inside my vagina*
Babysitter: *I really don't need to hear this*
and I'm supposed to be writing poetry

Wednesday, 10:09am, In the Forest

tips of trees
waving, You
hiding behind
some cusps of cloud

it smells like fall
when I was four
and jumped
in raked-up piles
and more

was faith-full

Wednesday, 10:09pm

What life-cherishing force (in women?) says "Yes!"
cannot resist the natural instinct cannot make our instincts
   act contrary to our instincts, that our counterinstincts, so to say,
   should act instead of, indeed, as, our instincts
what cruelty for such a chasm, such a choice:
either the *sole, undivided, genuine fulfillment, or, in other words....a child*
or the   *requirement, indeed demand...that the world... "must be described"*

how shall a (Jewish) woman navigate this incompatibility?

Friday, 11pm

I have crept into bed. The lapping dream
has welcomed me into her blue
waters. To be so awash in sleep
is precious; pearls of poems
glisten on the sandy floor
She got toothpaste all over my sink
I hate sharing a bathroom with her
I hate her - Mama? Were you sleeping?

Friday, 11:05pm - Saturday, 4:24am

Diving, diving,
for the pearls,
coming up
exhausted, empty-
handed...

Maya Bernstein

Saturday, 7:23am

I understand that just beyond
this kitchen where again I am
serving breakfast, the world
is awakening; the soft dawn
has yawned into sky, owls
have burrowed themselves
into their cool holes, fish
dart and flash and jump –
but someone has finished
the Honey Nut Cheerios
so someone else is crying
at the injustice – there goes summer
glory upon the trees, husky
greens, soaring corn,
fuzzy peaches, rowboat oars –
but I must calm the crisis,
must get them from pre-breakfast
to post-breakfast – I know
somewhere those black
bears are poking snouts into
blueberry brambles,
dappled fawns on awkward legs
are bending to lick the rushing
rivers, but I'm wiping down
the counters, wiping
away their tears, and the sun
has climbed too high
in that sky for me to poetry –

Saturday, 4:50pm, In the Forest

I found belief in this brief leaf

Fie the Skies of Doubts!

I'll cleave to these leaves

With my heart on my sleeve

As the wind howl-heaves about

Maya Bernstein

Saturday, 11:55pm

Re-reading Kertész

> ...it is precisely the untenability of our lives
> which leads to our flashes of recognition,
> in the light of which we come to recognize
> that our life is untenable - and it really is that,
> untenable, because it is taken away from us.

able to sleep only when
(and if) I know
they're asleep

Sunday, 8:18am

three tablespoons melted butter
mashed with an overripe banana
a cup of plain yogurt (Ella and Louis
singing *Summertime*) a farm-fresh egg –
whisk, mash, mix – a cup and a half of whole
wheat pastry flour, half a teaspoon of salt
– whisk, mash, mix – two of baking powder,
a few heaping spoonfuls of ground flax seeds;
make a well, circle that spoon, notice your body
dancing, nothing like dancing
in the morning kitchen
the house momentarily at peace
blackberries glistening in their azure
bowl, soon the smell wafts through the walls
soon they'll all come running, hungry,
bright, eager, we'll swing our hips, we'll
laugh, the taste of it all so sweet on the lips

Maya Bernstein

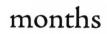

Prayer, After the Diagnosis

Pass over me,
though there is no blood
on my doorpost, though
I am not

at home but, like You,
in constant motion,
hoping to go unnoticed.

Not so much to smite
as to not be smitten.

There Is No Place Without You

> When they called to confirm the diagnosis
> I was in the parking lot at the zoo
> "No Caller I.D" – so couldn't tell who
> it was. I sent the kids ahead to the tortoises –
> the words sounded foreign. I had nowhere to record
> the acronyms, numbers, positive and negative
> signs; the worry in the voice was all I heard
> as I walked past where the snakes lived,
> the giraffes, the popping popcorn, and the lemurs:
> it was August. I was sweating. The tigers
> were nowhere to be found. The kids were disappointed.
>
> We passed a sign in Russian, *Ostorozhno!* I pointed:
> *Tigri Ryadom!* Beware! Tigers Near! So stay hopeful, I said,
> and felt them stalking me. I was full of dread.

Akeidah

This time,
not only
did I bring You
my innermost
hopes and fears,
my most fervent prayers,
my purest voice
lifted in song, tears
streaming down my cheeks,
but also my breasts.

I placed them
on Your crowded Altar,
squeezing them in
at the edge, and wondered
if the smell of the blood
and the milk and the smoke
rising heaven-ward
might be enough
for You,
this year.

Maya Bernstein

In Lot's Wife's Image

this treatment
has unsexed me
my sweat no longer
smells, pubic hair gone,
inner clock too, my moon
magnet my crampy companion
these thirty years, gone,
          my breasts
those breasts I did not want

at ten, I wanted
to freeze time
climb trees be
a boy; now, strangely
though a mother,
a wife, my dream's come
true, I look like her
but she sits
high in the branches
looking ahead
and I lean against the trunk
gazing back
at the trail
of blood and salt

18 Translations of a Line

"Hakol bidei shamayim chutz miyir'at shamayim"
—Babylonian Talmud, Brachot 33b

1. everything is in Your hands except for my belief in You
2. everything I perceive is my perspective
3. my skin is thin, slippery; I am what is left over of myself
4. everything (everything [in my control] everything) everything
5. nothing except interpretation
6. if x (where x = I believe) then y (and y = I'm more likely to feel safe)
7. nothing (nothing [fear] nothing) nothing
8. though I am alive, I am gutted
9. x-y (when x = I'm safe and y = except when I'm not)
10. everything floats cloudlike by; I impose shapes
11. my scars look like angry silent mouths, grimacing
12. (what remains of my body) > (praise)
13. -x + -y = z wherein x = I still believe in you, and y = I stopped believing in you and z = it doesn't matter
14.
15. I stand on my own shoulders reaching my hands towards You, since
16. everything in Heaven's hands. But You elude my grasp
17. when {I clench my fists with awe} then {fear slips through my fingers}
18. x (y-z) = xy - xz, in which x = You still believed in me, and y = You stopped believing in me and z = the numerical equivalent of spiritual gravity

There Is No Place Without You

The ring is thick and round, so wide
it fits
around three of my fingers.

My great-grandmother
Bina's hands
were already arthritic

when she was diagnosed
and had
the ring made, the Aramaic

phrase inscribed in the gold band
לית אתר פנוי מיניה
there is no place without you

her way of saying, *I believe,*
so spare me.
Her daughters fought

over who would inherit it.
My grandmother
gave it to my aunt, who gave it to me

on a gold chain to wear around my neck
during the chemo
infusions. Oh, this heavy inheritance. Oh,

why must you betroth yourself
to me
like this? It's obvious you've got me

in your grip. It's obvious
I'm wrapped
around your little finger.

A Rock is Not a Stone

[N]o things but in the sounds of the words representing them.
A rock is not a stone. But why is a rock not a stone?
 – Mary Oliver, *A Poetry Handbook*

There was a rock
    in my breast,
        not a stone.

It was a rock
    that was thrown,
        not a stone,
by young David.

        It struck Goliath
    between the eyes.
Just a stone's throw

            from boy to King,
    but it must have begun with
      a pouch of stones

gathered for other purposes, I imagine,
    for instance, him humming along
      a narrow river searching

    for stones to skip
along the banks,
    where still those
      rare flat precious stones

are eyed, desired,
    like I desire to overturn
      every stone,

Maya Bernstein

smooth myself over,
un-rock what's been rocked,
sing notes

of stones
un-thrown.

Sitting Shiva for my Estrogen

I really should make the time
        to sit Shiva for my estrogen.
But who would come to tell
        beautiful stories about her?
Certainly not my forsaken lover,
        and the children are glad
not to remember her at all, how
        slippery and round
she was, full of desire, always, how she would show
        up like an embarrassing relative
overflowing, unannounced,
        wearing a ridiculous hat
teeming with fuchsia
        hydrangeas, her heaving breath
preceding her perfume
        as she poured into the house. I should sit
and remember her better, but it's hard now
        to lower myself to the floor, to bend,
to twist, to gaze, to long, to stop
        hoping somehow she may yet come
just once more down the driveway.

There Is No Place Without You

Nothing is forgotten from before Your honored
throne. Nothing hidden from before Your seeing eyes.

Everything is exposed.   I too am known to You.
The sacks of my secrets   spilled beneath the shadow

of Your wings, the heaviness I've carried
since before You passed Your glory over my face

and chose me, and loved me, and desired me, and touched me
above my lips. Your milk so sweet upon my tongue.

They say that I forgot but I did not. My soul
indeed like dust to everyone. Your footprints too

upon my sands, the desert sands through which I drag
my feet and yes, I remember the lovingkindness

     of our youthful times. Praise us
         for daring not to forget. It rises

            before us as I call out to You,
            You who hears my cries.

       My insides churn at the thought
of us, as your mercy-womb envelops us.

Looking for a Bathroom in North Egremont, MA

I hoped the Inn across the street would say that I
     could use the loo. I really had to go,
but Frank at Ye Olde Country Store said, "Hi,
     so sorry, no." Outside an ancient oak,
with purple leaves and crumbling bark was rife
     with slimy caterpillars, festering and camouflaged
and clumped. There seemed to be a history of strife;
     the Innkeeper, his knife in hand, his kitchen full of aged
cheese and homemade jams and local ale, agreed
     to let me use his rosebud-scented stall only
if I swore to steer clear of Frank's store. Indeed, I did,
     and tried to hide my tracks. But as I made my lonely
way uphill I thought of Frank and of his blighted tree.
     It haunted me. It haunted me.

To Hug A Tree
for Olga

After your third round
      of chemotherapy, to counteract bad energy,
      it's good to hug a tree.
(It's not as simple or as silly as it seems –
      there is a courting, electricity, at play).
      No need to name the genus. Just lean
into the sap-like rays of slanting light
      (to stave off death).
      The tree calls out. Don't resist.
      Choose a tree gripping its leaves
      (to reduce hair loss).
            Place cheek on bark, rough on soft.
              The tangled roots below
as astounding as the hush above.
Stand. Flow. Let
the passersby gawk.
      Don't let go.

European Copper Beech

When I'm feeling down about the state of my body
      (for example, an MRI recently showed that I have scarring
      in my left frontal lobe, an old, hidden scar
           in addition to the new, visible
     scars on my breasts, and there's that time I fell
         off a brick wall when I was seven,
       add the knee, then all the children, so, my belly)
I take solace in the bumps and humps and lumps
       of the European Copper Beech.

Her twig-like branches
      as delicate as the white plastic wish-
          bone from Hasbro's Operation game,
her massive branches hang like the overflowing
      shopping bags of old ladies on buses, skin
      wrinkled   wrangled   wrought.

          I wonder
what intricate lymphatic system runs the course of these reaching limbs,
      what limbic system controls this tree's behavior
        and emotional responses, what to make
of the stubby toes at the base of her massive trunk.
      She sprouts tiny greens like unwanted hairs.
The circumference of her trunk alone is breathtaking.

    When I look up and up and still further up, one elegant bough
      looks like a pubescent girl with lengthy legs,
        a dark vagina, waifish waist,
           petite tree-knob breasts.

Another seems as frail as the forearm of an ancient
            woman I used to visit at the old age home across the street
                     from the synagogue in Palo Alto; she'd lay
           her warm hand on top of mine. Her bottom's
       studded with juttings like belly fat. *It looks like*
            (say the passers-by) *an old elephant.* When I was nine
            my family visited the San Diego zoo. The most
            enormous elephant was named Maya. *My daughter's*
            name is Maya! said my father. I was ashamed,
                but now I understand:
                    that elephant,
                       this tree,
                           me.
       Today the physical therapist moved my neck
all the way to the left. *There.*
     Your head is aligned now, it's straight,
     your nose in line with your belly button.
                Impossible, I thought
     but when I look at this tree which seems to teeter-
            totter and return to straightness, its flexible
            endless deviant erectness, aligned with itself,
    I lose my sense of "straight" and "line" and am comforted.

This perceptive physical therapist also noticed
           a strange extra pocket of skin near my armpit, *maybe it is a reservoir*
             of fat cells, or a pulled muscle, or sometimes
                when they have removed lymph nodes
                    this happens, she said.
  I walk around the world
    of this tree.
     I touch
    each clump,
      each wedge,
    each fatty knob,
     each scar,

I look up at her rustling copper skirt,
        a sea of red
blood cells. I think about how each month
        they insert a pine-like needle into
            whatever veins I have left
                that are still willing
      to offer their sacrifice, and squeeze out vials
      I would not have thought to call copper.

I sit and wait,
        and wait, for them
to come back with the counts. How could one count
        the leaves on this tree?

She seems so indifferent to me
        sitting here, loving her in my way, leaning
            into her, noticing, imagining
roots growing from under my tailbone, tunneling
        as deep and as wide as hers must,
            she, over 200 years old, she
                still rooted, still reaching.

Ghost Forest

The pigeons didn't seem to care
        which branches were alive.
They perched as if they could declare
        Nothing can survive.

Whole forests ghosted, suddenly
        gone. Leaves and roots and shoots,
ancient canopies
        poisoned by the brute

force of salt waters rising,
        soaking into silt.
The hollow trunks, sinking
        into dirt.

These forty-nine carcasses,
        giants with no pulse,
once grew, but now are charred
        ash: roasted, gutted, stuck.

Forgive the Nonsense of My Past Prayers

When you lose
your sense
of taste
and smell
the good disappears
too. Together with the bad.

I'm slathered in Vicks Vaporub and I reek, but don't feel bad
because I can't detect even a hint of camphor, or eucalyptus. I've lost
all gustation & olfaction. Not a fraction left. They disappeared
quickly; I didn't have the sense
to see it coming, but if I had I would have quickly smelled
my neighbor's beautiful basil that I pick in handfuls for pesto and tasted

the gazpacho to see if it needed more pepper. My tastes
have evolved over the years. On a bad
day I prefer a Bloody Mary to an ice cream cone. I smell
different too, more salty, more like the sea. But I've lost
my focus, which must dwell between nose and tongue. Mostly I'm incensed
at myself that for so long I implored that the pain in my life disappear;

I no longer want it to disappear.
What would the madeleine dipped in piping tea have tasted
like with faulty odor receptors? Scalding liquid and crumbs. The sensitivity
of our souls to the bitter, to the bad,
determines the sweetness of our bliss. How will I make up the lost
time? How will I recall these days in which I cannot smell

my shampooed hair after the shower, the smell
of a thunderstorm, drenched applewood, disappearing
smoke from the beeswaxed wick; it's like I've lost
my life-force. I want to taste
sour milk again, a rotten peach, a bad
egg, please, forgive the nonsense

Maya Bernstein

of my past prayers. I offer now this incense
on the smoldering altar: I want to smell
the terror, to hear the bad
news. Don't let the hardships disappear.
My tastes
have changed. I'm ready to face the loss.

Going 80 on the Taconic

After the last treatment. Late winter afternoon.
   Give me one reason to stay here, Tracy croons,

        all contralto, *and I'll turn right back
     around,* and the fender – suddenly smacked.

     Dusk + deer + snow + speed,
the startled deer darting across to feed

        or hide or nurse her fears or count the stars –
   and Orion's Belt has moved to my rearview. I'm at war

with God. Why does He always send some beast
    to block my path? Heading north instead

        of home, each passing car a portent
   of blinding brights. I finally see, I'm meant

   to be alive like this – alert, afraid – it's clear.
        I'm here, I'm here, I'm here.

years

Elul Ghazal

The new moon rises. I look beyond the windowsill, return
my gaze to God. Somewhere, a Shofar wails its cry, a shrill "Return!"

God, if You are King, I want to be Your Queen.
I'd write You love notes with my feathered quill, *Return...*

Come to my bed. If You're a shepherd, I want to be
a sheep leaping through the grassy hills, returning.

I'm Seeking You, Your staff and flask and flute and sandaled feet.
I hide in my chamber. You made a promise I expect You to fulfill: to return.

The sun glares through the window. I pull
the curtains closed. I stray in my heart, but still, I return.

I graze in the pastures of my dreams, I laze in my verdant bed, but
You've slipped from the linen sheets before I've had my fill, my turn.

I seek but cannot find You. I place a sachet of myrrh
between my breasts, hoping it will spill, return

Your hungry gaze toward me, so I will not stray
after the flocks of Your companions. I'll despair till You return.

Then will the trees put forth their fruit? Will turtle-
doves begin to coo? Will You hear my voice and thrill at my return?

If only You would whisper, *Maya, come to me!*
Your love is better than wine! Then I will return.

Routine Follow-Up

I stand in the thin cotton gown, opened to the front,
revealing myself. Last night I stood in this very same
position in my plush white terry robe,

smelling of jasmine, of avocado oil shampoo,
my nipples, which I'm lucky weren't sliced cleanly off me
like the calyx off a strawberry, beacons of beckoning

to my husband who let himself be rough,
his mouth swallowing me, his tongue slashing, a knife
buttering me with his saliva. Now I find myself standing

under fluorescent lights, the surgeon handing me a mirror
to hold as he dictates notes. I watch the reflection
of his fingers tapping expertly around the edges,

the upper lateral and lower quadrants, the posterior,
the implants neatly aligned behind my rosy areolas, shame-
red with survivor's guilt. I think of my husband's desire,

how I stared into the darkness as he caressed me,
just as I'm staring into this mirror I was made to hold,
my pupils searching for some reflection

of my own desire for myself.

Spec[tac]ular

Our love, it's spectacular. Our love is:
       a reflection of the sun

       bouncing off a mirror.
The window is: a bright

cold afternoon. I squint,
       unsure if it's good to look at you, if I'm

       at the center. I'm unsure – am I
who I am looking at you looking at

       who I am? Looking at you looking
at the center? I'm unsure. Am I

unsure if it's good to look at you? If I'm
       cold? Afternoon. I squint.

       The window is: a bright
bouncing off, a mirror,

a reflection of the sun,
       our love. It's spectacular, our love is.

Maya Bernstein

Desire as a Featherbed

I can't sleep – I might become wild.
I've been afraid of the satin sheets of nights

all my life. I was born wild –
but raised tame & trained, nights,

to be still in my cotton pajamas. Were
I to need something – water, touch – I

would float above myself, above the flesh & thirst. With
my eyes closed, I could imagine Thee,

O Kingdom of Sleep, thy gilded golden mirrors, featherbeds, wild-
patterned velvet piles, silken robes. How I desire those nights!

But in bed, I lie awake, wondering, what if I should
become feral, fierce? Who will I be if I be-

come capable of dreaming of linen, of lace? My
terror at the thought of surrender to such heavy luxury.

I Drift Towards Thoughts of You

Sea otters hold hands when they sleep
so they won't float away from each other.

> Sea horses may be the slowest
> of fish, but they hold each other's tails

when they swim; they live in pairs.
Adolescent ravens form gangs, then,

> two by two, they settle. And cows
> sleep standing up but only

dream when lying down. At night,
supine, I try to dream

> of you. By day I'm half asleep.
> I drift towards thoughts of you.

I want to be your gang, your pair,
to grab or hold some part

> of you that wags or waves
> or wavers in the wind, the wind

that blows past grasses
where the cows repose.

Our Intimacy

Our intimacy
has become

a privacy
I deprive

my most
intimates. I

intimate in
the light

of our
dark shrouded

secrecy, exposing
prior privation:

they are
not privy.

Why You Must Come Back to the City

When we are together we are
an exclamation, an obscurity, a meter.

No herd of cows or loveliness
of ladybugs or any gaggle of geese

could stop me trying to lure you home.
No bouquet of buttercups or dandelions

can compete with hot subway air,
and while we may not have brown bears

we do have pigeons. And reception.
Forget wrap-around porch perfection,

forget peaches, corn, sunflower seeds,
dispensaries of legal weed.

They have nothing over our fire-hydrants
and air conditioning. I just can't

face the heat without you. Come on,
I'm not asking you to amputate an arm.

Give up your mountain views!
Worship me in city pews!

A sparkle of fireflies
cannot pollute night's skies

like our light. Who needs stars
when we could stare, and stare...I dare

you: *come back*. (Alternatively, you might invite me
to be your guest in the country).

When I'm Without You

I'm as low as an owl
on the prowl. I glide

restless, my wings
are wind, all howl

about that hallowed
ground. This fallow mood,

so foul. I allow
my face a scowl.

I swallow, I wallow,
I'm hollow, in stealth –

in search – of you.
All alone,

low as an owl,
I become my own

prey. I growl
without a sound.

When I Peel an Orange

Western Massachusetts, 2021

I peel an orange.
The pith beneath my finger-
nails, my fingertips white.
It's sticky work
and I chew slowly,
section after section,
then realize: I'm not hungry
for the orange, rather
am hungry to tell
you about how I dig
my nails into its thick skin.
Open it. How fragrant I become.
How wet my lips
with juice. And though I'll wash
my hands and wipe
my face, it's the lingering
aroma of orange peel
on my fingers that I desire,
to make you turn your head,
flare your nostrils, open wide
your mouth and gape.

( )

Maya Bernstein

Minsk, Belarus, 1998

Holy Rabbis are buried in unmarked graves all over this land.
We stuffed psalm-books in our knapsacks and got in a long black
car driven by an ice-eyed tight-lipped Belarusian. We were taking
a day-long break from volunteering at a winter camp for Jewish
children from Minsk whose great-grandparents didn't
get on a boat in 1918 like mine. Wide-eyed children
whose parents shopped in supermarkets that had no eggs,
let alone citrus fruit, that December. (It was December).
I'd been there no more than a week. Had long run out
of the dumb snacks I'd brought from the U.S.: M&Ms,
Quaker Chewy Granola Bars, Trident Spearmint gum.
I subsisted on what they served the kids: *chai* — bitter
black tea; *bulochki* — sweet yeasty breakfast rolls; and *riba* —
thin slimy fish. Sometimes also *chesnok* — a raw garlic clove
or two, from the camp doctor's bulbous necklace.
She was never mocked, despite the stench.
When one of the religious boys in the front seat
took an orange from his bag and began to peel it,
I nearly fainted. He offered me a section but I turned my head
to look out the window at the cold fields of snow. To hide
my hunger. I imagined throwing his body from the moving car
 and eating that fat wet orange myself,
 the perfumed fruit's scent on my fingers.

( )

Ben Gurion Airport, Lod, 1983

The long-exiled Jews disembark.
They walk down the steep stairs
into the dizzying sunshine, into the bouquet
of a million blooming orange trees.
They become like juiced fruit, twisted,
reduced to pulp. It brings them to their knees.
That is why their lips

are close enough to kiss
the sacred ground.

( )

The Bronx, NY, 1947

Jewish immigrant women stand on the curb
in winter coats. Waiting for a delivery —
our girls — they call them, though
they have girls galore inside, spooning
hot soup from simmering stoves
in yeast-y, cinnamon-y, citrus-y
pith-redolent kitchens. The four
orange trees they are pacing
the icy pavement for are late,
but these are patient women,
turning over the problem
of how to keep the trees alive
while the ground is still frozen.

( )

Palm Springs, CA, 1991

My mother's tan feet on the dashboard, toes painted pale pink,
wriggling to the beat, my father driving, Paul Simon blasting, air
conditioning blowing, all of us in the rental-car-smelling rental car,
the three of us in the back, our thighs sticking to the seats, pushing
each other to move over, thirsty, one of us whines for a snack,
my mother pulls an orange from her bag, peels it in one long
tongue-like strip and dangles it, *if you'll be my bodyguard, I can be
your long-lost pal,* and I know that somewhere outside, in that wide
desert, snakes are shedding their skins and writhing away, and I want
to discard my orange peel self too, and slither through scorching
sands to my own cool rock, to pant in the shadows.

( )

Our Space, Nowhere, Everywhere, Now, Never, Always

...being with you...being with you...being with you...

I become   again
the child in the old song
        I peeled an orange
        I found inside
        Like in a nest
        A child asleep, a child asleep

The child in the song doesn't want to be found
        The child says: you made a hole here!
        Fix it! I'm getting cold, I'm getting cold.

But I do
want you
to find me.

You've discovered the hole
I've been hiding in and filled it
with your breath. I savor its honey-
juiced trail. Your words, your gaze
cannot leave me unpeeled.

But unlike that child, who
        Until this day,
        (If she hasn't caught a cold),
        Is sleeping, sleeping, in the orange,

I am awake, waiting
quietly in my nest, alert,
        waiting
for you   to be hungry,
to reach for me while I'm still moist.

I want to see your eyes
when you taste me.

Upon Entering St. John the Divine on a Sunny Afternoon

If my skin were stained glass
If my heart were a singing organ

If some maestro
Were found to sound

My clarion chords,
If the light shone just so –

Then my iridescence
Could spill into the nave, then

My hymns could suffuse the air
And the cathedral of me, myself

Could call to all
To come to worship

Lake Mansfield, 31 January

Summer-months, the waters warm when air is cool and cool when air is warm.
Now, this lake is frozen, January-solid beneath a boot-crunch of snow.

I lay my weight in the center. The sky's the same as when I floated here
some enveloping August afternoon ago. Still, I'm held. It's like learning you

again, after our spring, our summer, our fall
now, decades in, the ice, the frost –

but you don't crack. Still, you hold me, solid.
I'm safe with you like this: frozen, impenetrable, stolid.

There Is No Place Without You

My heart's a flopping fish that's caught
and you're the fisherman who says what's this
as round and round you turn me. I lie taut,
wriggling, gutted, cold. I want to be set
free. Wet. Waters washing over me and
flashing in the deep, un-caught, un-net-
ted, I will jump. And shine. And lure you from the sands
where slowly you will lower bait and rod,
trembling take a step or two toward
the blue. Your footprints left behind, unshod
bare feet awash in memory and desire.
Perhaps you'll turn into a fish like me—

You Have Returned My Soul to Me

I put my praise before You... for You have returned
my soul to me with compassion; abundant is Your faith
— Modeh Ani, a Jewish morning prayer

Perhaps it's wrong,
my confusing you
with God. But perhaps
I've been wrong,
all these years,
confusing God
with one like you,
who has returned
my soul to me, and more,
done it like a mother
bathing her infant.
My glossy head
an ostrich egg, speckled
in the palm of your clasping
long-boned hand. My spine
aligned along your inner arm
as you search my eyes, eyes
as wide as the gullet
of a wild chick's beak.
And when I cry out you dare
to meet my gaze, such
is the extent of your mercy.
But you don't stop there.
You smile, you coo, you sing
your song of faith:
how abundant is your faith
in me! I read recently:
The opposite of faith is not doubt,
but certainty. There's nothing
about you and me that is certain.

Each morning you undress
me, plunge me into
the waters of another day,
my soul the soap
you softly rub about my flesh.
I'm full of fragrant
potential in your hands.

Maya Bernstein

Notes

The phrase *There Is No Place Without You* is from the Zohar, 122b.

days

In "I'm Preparing My Body for Your Birth," *Hevre Kadisha* refers to volunteers who prepare a Jewish body for burial.

"Welcome to the Midst of the Mother That I Am" (as well as "Spec[tac]ular") are written in the specular form, created by the British poet Julia Copus.

"Imprisoned in Repetition and Immanence" uses language from Simon de Beauvoir's *The Second Sex*: "The domestic labors that fell to her lot because they were reconcilable with the cares of maternity imprisoned her in repetition and immanence; they were repeated from day to day in an identical form, which was perpetuated almost without change from century to century; they produced nothing new."

"Walking to Synagogue on Yom Kippur," borrows language from traditional Yom Kippur liturgy.

weeks

"Meditations on Incompatibility" includes multiple quotations from Imre Kertész's *Kaddish for an Unborn Child*.

months

The word *akeidah in* "Akeidah" means "sacrifice," and refers to the binding of Isaac as found in Genesis 19.

The original phrase in "18 Translations of a Line" comes from Tractate Brachot, 33b in the Babylonian Talmud, and can be translated as: *everything is in the hands of the Sky except for belief in the Sky.*

Maya Bernstein

"There Is No Place Without You" (Everything Is Exposed) borrows imagery from traditional Rosh HaShanah liturgy.

"Ghost Forest" is after Maya Lin's Installation in Madison Square Park's Conservancy, May-November 2021.

"Going 80 on the Taconic" includes lyrics from Tracy Chapman's song "Give Me One Reason" from her 1995 album *New Beginnings*.

years

Elul in "Elul Ghazal" refers to the last month of the Jewish calendar year, when the Shofar is blown each morning in preparation for the New Year. God is compared to a King who leaves the Palace to walk amongst the people.

"Desire as a Featherbed" is a Golden Shovel, a form created by the poet Terrance Hayes in homage to Gwendolyn Brooks. The last words of each line in the poem compose a complete stanza of Emily Dickinson's "Wild Nights."

"When I Peel An Orange" contains a reference to Paul Simon's song "You Can Call Me Al" from his 1986 album *Graceland*, and to Arik Einstein & Yoni Richter's song "Kilafti Tapuz" from their 1989 album *Pa'am Hayiti Yeled*.

In "Upon Entering St. John the Divine on a Sunny Afternoon," the phrase *me, myself* comes from Walt Whitman's *Leaves of Grass*, Section 4.

In "There Is No Place Without You" (My Heart's a Flopping Fish) the phrase "memory and desire" comes from the work of Wilfred Bion.

"You Have Returned My Soul to Me" owes a debt of gratitude to Sharon Olds' "Bathing the Newborn."

Acknowledgements

Thank you to the editors of the following publications for publishing the following poems, some in earlier forms:

Cider Press Review, "Routine Follow Up"
Eunoia Review, "Prayer, After the Diagnosis," "18 Translations of a Line," "Ghost Forest," "Lake Mansfield, 31 January," and "There Is No Place Without You (My Heart's a Flopping Fish)"
On the Seawall, "A Rock is Not A Stone," and "Walking to Synagogue on Yom Kippur"
Poetica Magazine, "I'm Preparing My Body for Your Birth"

I am deeply grateful to all who nurtured me – throughout this process, before it, and beyond it:

- Larry Yudelson for his belief in this manuscript, and Julia Knobloch for her sharp editorial eye and kind spirit
- Grace Schulman who led me to Yerra Sugarman who led me to Jehanne Dubrow
- Yerra, whose support and encouragement has been like rain to a ranunculus
- Jehanne, master of form in all forms, whose sharp eye and ear helped organize and shape this manuscript
- Zohar Atkins, Rachel Barenblat, Merle Feld, Judy Katz, and Alicia Jo Rabins - for your advice and guidance
- Anthony Anaxagorou and the members of the London Poetry School's Advanced Poetry Class 2020-2021
- My teachers past (Mr. Ira Berkowitz, z"l) and present, Marie Howe, R.A Villanueva, D. Nurske, Afaa Michael Weaver; and my fellow students in Sarah Lawrence College's MFA in Writing program
- Marty Linsky: mentor, cheerleader, friend
- My dedicated, generous, talented medical team
- Cecily Oberstein, Rachel Milner Gillers, Ellie Schainker, and Ora Weinberg for sticking close by no matter what,

and for reading early drafts; Sarah Mali and Celeste Villalobos Tahamont for helping me dance at the edge; Tova Speter, for agitating the artist in me

+ My family, Josh, Kyra & Dov, Shera & Alan, Ari & Liora, Micole & Oren, Andy, Opa & Anyu (z"l), Abigail, Yair & Ilana, Eliav & Adi – thank you for having my back, my neck, my head, for being my 911, 411, and 311

+ My parents, Gaya & Lewis, for your enduring loving support, and especially my mother, for instilling in me a love of poetry and words

+ My children, Ananya, Shefa, Erez, Niva, Boaz: there is no place without you

+ Noam, my first and last reader, with all these small steps and slow bites, look how far we've come

About the Author

Maya Bernstein's writing has appeared in the *Cider Press Review*, the *Harvard Business Review*, *On the Seawall*, *Poetica Magazine*, the *Stanford Social Innovation Review*, *Tablet Magazine*, and elsewhere. She is on faculty at Georgetown University's Institute for Transformational Leadership, the Masa Leadership Center, and Yeshivat Maharat. In 2012, Maya was awarded the Covenant Foundation's Pomegranate Prize for emerging leaders in the Jewish community. She holds a B.A in Russian Language and Literature from Columbia College, an M.Ed from Harvard's Graduate School of Education, and is a recipient of the Jane Cooper Fellowship at Sarah Lawrence College, where she is pursuing an MFA in Poetry. Maya's debut album, "Shiviti," with Noah Solomon, was released in 2021. She grew up in New York City and Jerusalem, and lives in Yonkers, NY with her family.

The Jewish Poetry Project

Ben Yehuda Press

From the Coffee House of Jewish Dreamers: Poems of Wonder and Wandering and the Weekly Torah Portion by Isidore Century

"Isidore Century is a wonderful poet. His poems are funny, deeply observed, without pretension." – *The Jewish Week*

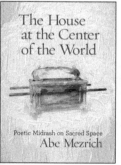

The House at the Center of the World: Poetic Midrash on Sacred Space by Abe Mezrich

"Direct and accessible, Mezrich's midrashic poems often tease profound meaning out of his chosen Torah texts. These poems remind us that our Creator is forgiving, that the spiritual and physical can inform one another, and that the supernatural can be carried into the everyday."
—Yehoshua November, author of *God's Optimism*

we who desire: Poems and Torah riffs by Sue Swartz

"Sue Swartz does magnificent acrobatics with the Torah. She takes the English that's become staid and boring, and adds something that's new and strange and exciting. These are poems that leave a taste in your mouth, and you walk away from them thinking, what did I just read? Oh, yeah. It's the Bible."
—Matthue Roth, author, *Yom Kippur A Go-Go*

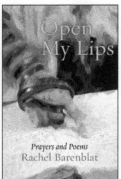

Open My Lips: Prayers and Poems
by Rachel Barenblat

"Barenblat's God is a personal God—one who lets her cry on His shoulder, and who rocks her like a colicky baby. These poems bridge the gap between the ineffable and the human. This collection will bring comfort to those with a religion of their own, as well as those seeking a relationship with some kind of higher power."
—Satya Robyn, author, *The Most Beautiful Thing*

Words for Blessing the World: Poems in Hebrew and English by Herbert J. Levine

"These writings express a profoundly earth-based theology in a language that is clear and comprehensible. These are works to study and learn from."
—Rodger Kamenetz, author, *The Jew in the Lotus*

Shiva Moon: Poems by Maxine Silverman

"The poems, deeply felt, are spare, spoken in a quiet but compelling voice, as if we were listening in to her inner life. This book is a precious record of the transformation saying Kaddish can bring. It deserves to be read. These are works to study and learn from."
—Howard Schwartz, author, *The Library of Dreams*

is: heretical Jewish blessings and poems by Yaakov Moshe (Jay Michaelson)

"Finally, Torah that speaks to and through the lives we are actually living: expanding the tent of holiness to embrace what has been cast out, elevating what has been kept down, advancing what has been held back, reveling in questions, revealing contradictions."
—Eden Pearlstein, aka eprhyme

Texts to the Holy: Poems
by Rachel Barenblat

"These poems are remarkable, radiating a love of God that is full bodied, innocent, raw, pulsating, hot, drunk. I can hardly fathom their faith but am grateful for the vistas they open. I will sit with them, and invite you to do the same."
—Merle Feld, author of A Spiritual Life.

The Sabbath Bee: Love Songs to Shabbat
by Wilhelmina Gottschalk

"Torah, say our sages, has seventy faces. As these prose poems reveal, so too does Shabbat. Here we meet Shabbat as familiar housemate, as the child whose presence transforms a family, as a spreading tree, as an annoying friend who insists on being celebrated, as a woman, as a man, as a bee, as the ocean."
—Rachel Barenblat, author, The Velveteen Rabbi's Haggadah

All the Holes Line Up: Poems and Translations
by Zackary Sholem Berger

"Spare and precise, Berger's poems gaze unflinchingly at—but also celebrate—human imperfection in its many forms. And what a delight that Berger also includes in this collection a handful of his resonant translations of some of the great Yiddish poets." —Yehoshua November, author of God's Optimism and Two World Exist

How to Bless the New Moon: The Priestess Paths Cycle and Other Poems for Queens
by Rachel Kann

"To read Rachel Kann's poems is to be confronted with the possibility that you, too, are prophet and beloved, touched by forces far beyond your mundane knowing. So, dear reader, enter into the 'perfumed forcefield' of these words—they are healing and transformative."
—Rabbi Jill Hammer, co-author of The Hebrew Priestess

Into My Garden: Prayers
by David Caplan

"The beauty of Caplan's book is that it is not polemical. It does not set out to win an argument or ask you whether you've put your tefillin on today. These gentle poems invite the reader into one person's profound, ambiguous religious experience."
—*The Jewish Review of Books*

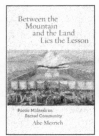

Between the Mountain and the Land is the Lesson: Poetic Midrash on Sacred Community by Abe Mezrich

"Abe Mezrich cuts straight back to the roots of the Midrashic tradition, sermonizing as a poet, rather than ideologue. Best of all, Abe knows how to ask questions and avoid the obvious answers."
—Jake Marmer, author, *Jazz Talmud*

NOKADDISH: Poems in the Void
by Hanoch Guy Kaner

"A subversive, midrashic play with meanings—specifically Jewish meanings, and then the reversal and negation of these meanings."
—Robert G. Margolis

An Added Soul: Poems for a New Old Religion
by Herbert Levine

"These poems are remarkable, radiating a love of God that is full bodied, innocent, raw, pulsating, hot, drunk. I can hardly fathom their faith but am grateful for the vistas they open. I will sit with them, and invite you to do the same."
—Merle Feld, author of *A Spiritual Life*.

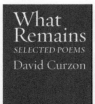

What Remains
by David Curzon

"Aphoristic, ekphrastic, and precise revelations animate What Remains. In his stunning rewriting of Psalm 1 and other biblical passages, Curzon shows himself to be a fabricator, a collector, and an heir to the literature, arts, and wisdom traditions of the planet."
—Alicia Ostriker, author of *The Volcano and After*

The Shortest Skirt in Shul
by Sass Oron

"These poems exuberantly explore gender, Torah, the masks we wear, and the way our bodies (and the ways we wear them) at once threaten stable narratives, and offer the kind of liberation that saves our lives."
—Alicia Jo Rabins, author of *Divinity School*, composer of *Girls In Trouble*

Walking Triptychs
by Ilya Gutner

These are poems from when I walked about Shanghai and thought about the meaning of the Holocaust.

Book of Failed Salvation
by Julia Knobloch

"These beautiful poems express a tender longing for spiritual, physical, and emotional connection. They detail a life in movement—across distances, faith, love, and doubt."
—David Caplan, author, *Into My Garden*

Daily Blessings: Poems on Tractate Berakhot
by Hillel Broder

"Hillel Broder does not just write poetry about the Talmud; he also draws out the Talmud's poetry, finding lyricism amidst legality and re-setting the Talmud's rich images like precious gems in end-stopped lines of verse."
—Ilana Kurshan, author of *If All the Seas Were Ink*

The Red Door: A dark fairy tale told in poems
by Shawn Harris

"THE RED DOOR, like its poet author Shawn C. Harris, transcends genres and identities. It is an exploration in crossing worlds. It brings together poetry and story telling, imagery and life events, spirit and body, the real and the fantastic, Jewish past and Jewish present, to spin one tale." —Einat Wilf, author, *The War of Return*